BE TRUE TO YOU

BE TRUE TO YOU

A PRACTICAL GUIDE TO PURSUING AN AUTHENTIC PATH

◆ ◆ ◆

Ruthann M. Wilson

ISBN 13: 9780692691540
ISBN 10: 0692691545
Library of Congress Control Number: 2016906255
In-Progress, LLC, Evanston, IL

CONTENTS

Acknowledgments

◆ ◆ ◆

I EXTEND GRATITUDE TO EVERYONE who has shared knowledge, wisdom, and experience about pursuing an authentic path.

I extend heartfelt thanks to my family and friends for their love and support. I especially thank Nelson for his patience, encouragement, and unwavering belief in me.

I thank Destiny for the honor of fostering her magical journey from caterpillar to butterfly. It was a great reminder to trust the process.

INTRODUCTION

◆ ◆ ◆

PRAYING BY MOONLIGHT

I AM AWAKENED BY ANOTHER dream.

I lie in bed, immersed in my own darkness.

I turn toward the window and see the moon shining brightly in the sky. I am comforted by its presence. It reminds me of the night-light in my bedroom when I was a child—just enough light to make the darkness bearable.

I pray for guidance.

I hear a whisper: "Embrace the darkness; it will lead you to the light."

I trust. I sleep. I awaken. And so it is.

◆ ◆ ◆

"Praying by Moonlight" reflects a time in my life when I felt lost and stuck in the past. The whisper I heard so clearly was my spiritual voice of truth. I had not listened to it for a very long time. I had allowed external voices to become more important than my own voice of truth. It was a pattern that began when I was young, and it resulted in me living my life for many years from a core belief that I was fundamentally flawed.

I became extremely self-conscious of my way of being at a very early age. I was frequently referred to as "quiet" and "shy" in a way that felt belittling. I would cringe every time I heard people describe me in that way. I felt misunderstood and unappreciated by people whose opinions I valued.

It was my perception that being quiet and more internally oriented was something I needed to overcome to be "normal" and accepted. The problem was that I did not know any other way to be. It was (and still is) who I am by nature.

From the outside looking in, I was seen as a quiet and shy child—stereotypically introverted, and yet I did not feel typical at all. I was a deep thinker in search of context for my life. I also had an incredible mystical life through my dreams.

I tried to overcome my introversion for many years to be seen as "normal" and to fit in; however, I was never able to overcome it. The second I would hear "She is so quiet" in reference to me, I knew I was failing at reinventing myself. I could not escape the label. It was true. I hated the label, and I hated me. It still saddens me to think that I could feel so much hatred toward myself.

I did not act out in response to what I was feeling; instead, I got even quieter. I was so incredibly quiet at one point in my life that my oldest sister fondly nicknamed me Miss Mouse. What she did not know was that I felt alone, isolated, and misunderstood living in my own world.

This was also a source of concern for my mother. She was afraid that people were going to take advantage of my quiet and easygoing nature. I did not completely understand the concept of being taken advantage of, but it did not sound good. Her concern became my concern, and I started building walls to protect myself.

My insecurity began to haunt me at night through my dreams. I often experienced situations in which I felt extremely vulnerable. I frequently found myself being chased, watched, or physically harmed.

Sadly, I did not talk about my dreams with anyone. I chose to suffer in silence. I did not want to be judged any further, and by that point, I was doing a pretty good job of judging myself anyway. I was completely uncomfortable in my own skin.

I concluded that I was fundamentally flawed and broken beyond repair. I allowed this belief to define me and bind me to a negative self-image for many years. My negative self-image influenced many choices I made for my life.

As I look back, I can see that my life lacked true intention and commitment to anything other than fitting in, following other people's agendas, and burying the pain of feeling inherently flawed.

Although I had a desire to grow beyond the limited view I had of myself, I was unable to overcome even deeper feelings of being flawed and not fitting in.

I worked hard to be a part of the norm. I was outwardly successful by following the path of least resistance but inwardly feeling as if a piece of me were dying each day. I was not pursuing my own dreams or expressing the creative part of myself on a consistent basis. I did not have the inner strength or confidence to regularly bring that part of me forward. It takes courage and confidence to continue to bring your true self forward as you grow and evolve.

Over time, the conflict of wanting to pursue my dreams and feeling held back by a limiting belief created a deep sense of sorrow. I felt like I was sinking into a deep, dark hole from which I would never escape.

I reached a point in my life where I had to explore the inescapable sorrow that lingered in my soul. I withdrew from the external world as much as I could and spent time alone reading books on spirituality and Jungian psychology. I journaled, reflected, and prayed.

I also started paying more attention to my dreams, writing them down and discussing them in the safety of a dream circle—a group of like-minded individuals who come together to support one another in remembering and exploring their dreams. I wanted to get back to a place of embracing my dreams as a source of information and inspiration the way I had done when I was younger.

It was during this time that I experienced the most profound dream of my life. It resulted in a spiritual awakening that proved to be a turning point.

Words can never describe or capture the experience of a dream. My intention in sharing my dream is to highlight the transforming power of truth and openness to spiritual guidance.

Dream

I was frustrated that I was not getting the results that I was seeking through the personal development work that I was doing.

I prayed for guidance as to what I needed to do to truly move my life forward. My guidance came to me in a dream in which I *vividly* and *intensely* experienced my younger self.

She appeared in my dream in distress and in need of my help. I was distracted and despondent over something else going on in the dream. I was frantically searching for our family's dog that I thought I had neglected. I sincerely love dogs, so the thought that I had neglected our dog was heartbreaking to me.

After a long and unproductive search through many clutter-filled rooms, I came upon a room that was empty except for a bed.

I sat on the edge of the bed and began to cry and mourn the loss of the dog. Shortly thereafter, the energy of the room changed, and my younger self appeared in the doorway holding her stomach. She said she did not feel well and needed my help.

The energy that she brought into the room was like nothing I had ever experienced before; it was palpable. Her energy was warm and profoundly loving despite the fact that she was in distress.

I told her I did not know how to help her. I felt guilty the second the words left my mouth, but it was true. I did not know how to assist her, and I was so emotionally drained by that point that I did not even want to get involved. I just wanted her to go away.

I awakened from this dream with an even deeper sense of sorrow. I cried every time I thought about my response to my younger self standing in the doorway asking for assistance. I could not believe I had refused to give her a hand.

I knew my dream was significant because the feelings that I had in the dream stayed with me for weeks thereafter. I was not able to talk about the dream without getting emotional.

I shared my dream with the dream circle that I was attending at the time. One of the members encouraged me to just sit with my feelings and allow them to inform me. He could tell it was an emotionally charged dream for me.

I took his suggestion to heart. I sat with my feelings for several weeks before I was able to understand the deeper meaning. I initially felt guilty for not being willing to help my younger self. What I came to realize is that she was actually there to help me. Through my dream, I was forced to admit the truth. I did not know how to help myself. I did not know how to truly liberate myself from a deep-seated childhood belief. My admission of the truth was an act of surrender, a yielding of control, which proved to be a major turning point in my life.

I reawakened to the part of me that guides and connects me to a higher plan and purpose. That part of me was always there. I needed to reawaken to it. Telling the truth was the key that opened the door to assistance from a higher place.

This reawakening helped me shift the disempowering belief that I was fundamentally flawed to a more empowering belief that I have a divine design that includes the gift of introversion—an innate ability to be self-reflective, introspective, and insightful. I learned to embrace the aspect of myself that I thought was a fundamental flaw as a part of a greater plan and purpose. I stopped trying to fix myself and started exploring what was true for me from a spiritual perspective.

I began to listen more closely to my spiritual voice of truth. It became clear to me that the way forward was through self-knowledge, self-acceptance, and *trust* that my steps were being divinely guided.

I began to cultivate a spiritual way of life through the principles and practices that I will outline in this book. I think of this way of life as walking a spiritual path.

Walking is a natural activity that is grounding; it connects us with the earth and brings us into present time. Being grounded and present is necessary for us to manifest our hopes and dreams. Walking is also an activity that takes us from one place to another at a pace that allows us to enjoy the journey. I believe that life is a journey that is intended to be enjoyed. Thinking of life as a journey helps us maintain a sense of wonder and adventure.

Spirituality is awareness/consciousness of a higher presence working in and through our lives. It is experienced as a sense of belonging to something greater, timeless, and infinite in possibility.

Cultivating your spirituality will provide you with a greater context for living your life and awaken you to the interconnectedness of all life. You will learn to live your personal truth in the context of universal truth. You cultivate your spirituality through a commitment to spiritual values, spiritual practices, and consistent action.

Ideals such as truth, freedom, unity, peace, kindness, and joy are examples of spiritual values. They are enduring principles and qualities that we bring to life through commitment and action. They are principles and qualities that elevate us individually and collectively.

Prayer, gratitude, forgiveness, and spending time in nature are examples of practices that increase spiritual awareness and openness to guidance. You may be surprised to see spending time in nature as a spiritual practice. It is important for us to remember that we are intimately connected to nature and depend on its cycles for our growth and well-being. We are in the flow of life when we are consciously connected to the cycles of life that sustain us.

There is no right or wrong way to walk a spiritual path. It is a deeply personal path that is influenced by your beliefs, trust, experiences, introspection, reflection, and practices. It is an internal process of discerning what is true for you and living from that truth.

This book is designed to help you explore what is true for you and put it into action, one day at a time. It is focused on personal development with a higher purpose in mind.

I believe in a spiritual source. I refer to this source as "God" in this book. That said, I am not promoting a particular path or religious tradition. I recognize and respect that you may have a different name for your spiritual source.

OVERVIEW OF THE BOOK

Chapter 1, "Be Intentional," is designed to help you embrace your power and explore your purpose through your values, gifts/talents, passions, and abilities.

Chapter 2, "Be Fruitful," is designed to help you assess where you are in your life and create a compelling future through value-based goals.

Chapter 3, "Be Thankful," highlights the gift of grace and the transformative power of gratitude.

Chapter 4, "Be Willing to Let Go," focuses on the power of releasing/letting go of what no longer serves you in order to make room for new beginnings, new opportunities, and new blessings.

Chapter 5, "Be Still," highlights powerful tools of self-renewal.

Chapter 6, "Bring It All Together on a Daily Basis," provides a framework to bring the principles and practices to life on a daily basis.

In the spirit of exploration, I have included questions within each chapter as well as suggestions to enrich your path. I encourage you to work through all of the questions. The goal is to deepen self-knowledge through an exploratory process.

I recommend that you have a notebook or journal handy to capture your thoughts and work through the questions and exercises. You may want to consider creating a regular journal practice as a part of this process. I have found my journal to be an invaluable tool for recording my dreams, clarifying my thoughts, and processing my feelings. It has also helped me to see how much I have grown over time.

In a spirit of authenticity, I have shared personal stories throughout the book. There may be parts of my stories that resonate with you. If so, I hope they inspire you to continue on your own unique path, be true to yourself, and to share your experiences with others.

This book is a relatively quick read if that is all that you do. It is an inner journey of discovery and outer expression of your authentic self if you commit to working through the questions/exercises and employing the practices as a part of your daily routine.

If any of the following statements resonate with you, please read on.

* I am seeking purpose and direction for my life.
* I feel stuck in one or more areas of my life.
* I have a hard time seeing beyond my current circumstances.
* I feel less than confident in my ability to make changes in my life.
* I am not living up to my potential in one or more areas of my life.

CHAPTER 1

BE INTENTIONAL

◆ ◆ ◆

POWER AND PURPOSE

THE WORD *INTENTION* COMES FROM the Latin word *intendere*, which means "to stretch out," "to extend." Your life's purpose is intended for your growth. It takes inner strength and confidence to bring your purpose to life.

POWER

The nature of life is change and transition for the purpose of growth and evolution.

The freedom to choose what is best for our own lives is one of our greatest powers and means of transforming our lives. It is essential power for our individual growth process.

Freedom/free will is a spiritual gift and a birthright. It is a right that enables each of us to pursue an authentic path. One's spirit, the very essence of one's being, is free. It cannot be bound by time, matter, or circumstance.

Freedom is a spiritual gift to be cherished and a right that should be secured for all. It is hard to believe that in this day and age, people are still fighting for basic freedom. I hold freedom of thought, speech, and expression for everyone as a prayer in my heart.

Freedom is a mind-set that manifests in our lives through choices and action.

We often give our power away through indecision or indifference, and that can undermine our self-worth and self-confidence.

If you are not living your own conscious choices, you are living someone else's choices for you, and that may or may not be in your best interest.

You step into your power one decision at a time. You lose power every time you allow someone else to make a decision for you that you are capable of making for yourself.

We create our lives (and world) every day through the choices that we make. The challenge is that we often move so quickly through the day that we do not pause to think about the seemingly small choices that shape the future for better or worse. Decisions that we made yesterday are impacting our lives today.

We each have to decide who or what is a source of power for our lives. The most common sources of power that people seek are money and positions of influence. These are examples of external sources of power that are subject to external conditions to remain power sources. As external conditions change (e.g., change in the value of the dollar, loss of a job), so does our power.

Spiritual power is true power that comes from within. It is fueled by a deep sense of connection to your personal freedom and self-worth. It is not subject to external conditions to be a source of power.

When we are powered from inside out, external sources of power such as financial wealth and positions of influence become vehicles through which we contribute versus vehicles through which we seek power.

When we live our lives from inside out, we know that we are free to choose our own path—that we have inherent worth. We know that we are part of something greater and that we have something unique and important to bring into the world.

When we live our lives from the outside in, our personal freedom is always at risk and our self-worth is tied to other people's perception of our worth, the amount of money we make, the positions we hold, and the possessions we own.

Spiritual power is experienced as inner strength and confidence to choose what is best for your own life. It is true power that comes from within. No one can give it to you, and no one can take it away either. You have to claim it for yourself. It is an ongoing process of embracing and living your personal truth.

Knowing who you are and what is most important to you will provide you with the clarity to make empowering choices for your life.

Your choices reveal your true beliefs. If you are making choices that are contrary to what you say you want for your life, you probably have hidden or unacknowledged beliefs that need to be explored.

Do you have a goal that always seems to be out of reach? What choices have you made with respect to the goal? Are your choices supportive or unsupportive of what you are trying to achieve?

Choices that are unsupportive of your goals are clues that there are hidden or unacknowledged beliefs that are most likely rooted in doubt and/or fear about something or someone. There may be feelings of not being worthy of a goal, not believing a goal is attainable, fear of failure, or even fear of success. It might seem strange to list success as a fear, but it can hold you back if you fear losing something as a result of success (e.g., a successful career at the expense of the family) or you fear that you will not be able to maintain a certain level of success on an ongoing basis.

Once you bring light to your hidden or unacknowledged beliefs, you can release them and replace them with beliefs that empower you to pursue what you truly desire.

Embrace your power through choices that affirm your personal freedom and self-worth.

Questions for Reflection

What are you choosing for your life? Why?

Who or what is a source of power for your life? Why?

What choice can you make today to step into your power?

Why would this choice help you step into your power?

Connecting with your inner power is necessary to bring your purpose to life. It will energize you and enable you to persevere despite obstacles and setbacks along the way.

PURPOSE

Do you believe that you were created with a purpose in mind? I hope the answer to the question is a resounding *yes* even if you do not feel a strong sense of purpose and direction right now.

I spent a number of years unsuccessfully "looking" for my purpose. What I came to realize is that we do not need to "look" for purpose; purpose is built into our being. We come into the world equipped to build a meaningful, purposeful, and abundant life.

We have a divine design that includes values, gifts/talents, passions, and abilities that are waiting to be explored and brought to life.

- ❀ Values are principles and qualities that are most important to you.
- ❀ A gift/talent is something that comes naturally to you whether or not you have fully developed it.
- ❀ Passion is desire/enthusiasm for something or someone.
- ❀ Ability is the potential that you have to make choices, solve problems, develop skills, and so on.

I believe that we create a life of meaning and purpose through self-knowledge, self-acceptance, inner guidance, commitment, and action. Our lives are intended to unfold from inside out.

We have a number of great examples of purpose-driven lives over the course of history—Jesus, Mohandas Gandhi, Dr. Martin Luther King Jr., Nelson Mandela, and Mother Teresa, just to name a few.

If you study the lives of the people listed above, you will find a deep sense of commitment to spiritual values such as freedom, unity, and unconditional love as well as a deep sense of connection to a spiritual source.

You will also find that all of them faced obstacles and challenges as they brought their values to life through teaching, healing, fighting for independence, standing up for civil rights, and caring for the sick and poor. Obstacles and challenges were a part of the process and challenged each one of them to stretch and grow.

People often think that if they are living "on purpose," their lives will be problem-free. Living a purposeful life is not without challenges; however, when we are motivated by something we care about deeply, we persevere despite challenges and setbacks. It is through life's challenges that we stretch, grow, and deepen our faith in divine possibility.

The nature of life is change and transition for the purpose of growth and evolution. On a personal level, growth and evolution relates to your soul (or mind). Your soul, in essence, is your personality. It is comprised of thoughts, beliefs, feelings, experiences, and memories. It is the mental and emotional levels of your being.

Your soul grows and evolves over the course of a lifetime. It is your individuality, and it makes you uniquely you. There never has been and never will be anyone exactly like you. Please take a minute and internalize the idea that there never has been and never will be anyone exactly like you.

Your purpose is intended for your soul's growth and your contribution to the greater good. I believe that we are here to do our "work" on a soul level with the goal of being spiritually guided.

Your soul seeks individuality; your spirit seeks the highest good for all. As such, personal development work in a spiritual context will enable you to live your life with a higher purpose in mind.

I used examples of well-known people to illustrate the power of being purpose driven. Not everyone is intended to live out his or her purpose on the world's stage; however, that does not make your reason for being any less important or impactful on a smaller scale.

People often think their purpose is defined by a job or a career. It is not. Your purpose transcends a job, role, or position. These are vehicles through which you live your purpose; however, they are not your purpose.

Your purpose is not a one-time event. It manifests over the course of your lifetime in various ways. As an example, I have a friend who has inspiration as a part of his purpose. It is reflected every day through the interactions he has with his kids, coworkers, friends, and even strangers. Inspiration is a part of his character and everyday life. He is also a great storyteller. I expect that he will inspire others through speeches and books when he is ready to embrace that part of his journey.

Exploring your divine design with an open heart and mind can bring light as to your purpose and potential. It will help you understand who you are and what you are here to do.

We often have a sense of what we are here to do, but we are afraid to claim it, because it will require us to make changes that will take us out of our comfort zone. Embracing your purpose will take you out of your comfort zone. It is intended to help you stretch, grow, and deepen your faith in divine possibility.

I suggest that you begin exploring your purpose by identifying and clarifying your values. Your values are the foundation of your life. They inform your life choices and help you set priorities for your life. For example, if you are someone who has natural beauty as a core value, you are likely to make different life choices (e.g., where you live, how you live, how you present yourself) than someone who does not have natural beauty as a core value.

When you are living your life according to your values, you are being true to yourself and others. There is congruence between what you think, what you say, and what you do. Conversely, when you do not know who you are and what is important to you, you will allow other people and situations to define you and direct your life.

You will want to spend time identifying and clarifying your values so that you are crystal clear as to what you are seeking for your life. Clarification will help you have a spiritual end in mind. For example, if I was coaching someone, and that person listed money as a value, I would encourage him or her to dig deeper in terms of what money means to him or her. Money is not a value. It is a means to something that is valued such as independence or philanthropy. You will want to be sure that you have captured the higher/end value as you finalize your list of foundational values.

Generally speaking, money and possessions are means to something that you value in your life. Think about how you spend your money and what possessions you currently own. It will provide insight as to what you value in your life. If you are not able to connect a possession with a personal value, it may be time to let it go. The ability to let go of things that no longer bring you joy or serve your highest good is an important spiritual practice that we will discuss later in the book.

Getting clear on who you are and what is important to you will help you create a life that is true to you. Your spiritual heart is your center of truth and authenticity. It is your guide to living to your highest potential.

You invoke the wisdom of the heart when you ask yourself questions such as, "What is true for me?" "What is true about this situation?" "What is true about my life?" "What is true about life?" *Truth* is the light that guides your way.

The following questions and exercises are provided to engage your inner wisdom and help you explore what is true for you. They are best accomplished in writing and with an open heart and mind.

I encourage you to take your time answering the questions and working through the exercises. Explore the underlying reasons for each of your answers for deeper insight. Look for themes and patterns in your responses. Your responses to these questions and exercises will be used in the next chapter.

> Your vision will become clear only when you
> look into your heart. Who looks outside,
> dreams. Who looks inside, awakens.

> — CARL JUNG

EXPLORE WHAT IS TRUE FOR YOU
Identify, clarify, and prioritize your values (principles and qualities that are important to you). This is a critical exercise for building a life that is true to you.

Orienting your life around spiritual values will elevate your life and pull you forward.

Examples of Values:

Authenticity	Connection	Organization
Integrity	Peace	Compassion
Unity	Learning	Creativity
Joy	Fulfillment	Adventure
Loyalty	Experience	Empowerment
Contribution	Abundance	Simplicity
Freedom	Truth	Beauty
Excellence	Balance	Nature

* Identify eight to ten values that are most important to you.
* Clarify what each value means to you, why it is important, and how it is or will be expressed in your life.
* Prioritize the list of values.
* Your top three to five values or value strings are the foundational layer for your life.
  o Value strings are words that are closely related such as integrity/trust, freedom/independence, and truth/authenticity.

The goal is to identify values that resonate with you.

* I value...

You will find that you are already living many of your values. The process of clarifying and prioritizing your values enables you to see where you are being true to yourself and where you might need to make adjustments. Honoring your values is an act of self-love and self-care.

❋ I need to adjust...

Identify three to five words that describe who you are at your core. Positive "I am" statements are extremely powerful in building your self-esteem. Experiment with different words until you find three to five words that resonate with you.

❋ I am...

Write a few words that describe what you feel you are here on earth to do.

❋ I am here to...

Identify your passions.

❋ I feel passionate about...
❋ My greatest desire is to...

Identify what comes naturally to you (e.g., writing, singing, organizing, storytelling, etc.).

❀   I naturally…

Identify your skills/areas of expertise.

❀   I am skilled at…

Identify lessons you are here on earth to learn.

❀   I am here to learn…

Describe how you define success and why you define it in this way.

❀   Success is…

What have been some of the most meaningful times in your life? Why have they been meaningful?

❀   The most meaningful times in my life have been…

What would you miss the most in your life if it were no longer available to you? Why would you miss it?

❀   I would miss…

If you had to choose one word for your tombstone that best describes your essence, what would it be? Why this word?

❀   The word that would best describe my essence is…

How would a good friend describe you? If you do not know the answer to the question, ask.

❀   My good friend would describe me as…

How do you want to change the world? Why?

❀   I want to change the world…

In what areas have you been inspired to serve others? Why these areas?

❀   I have been inspired to serve others through…

Who or what is a source of strength for you? Why?

❀   My greatest source of strength is…

Who do you admire? Why? These are mirror qualities. You are not able to recognize qualities in others that you do not possess.

❀   The person I admire the most is…

Sometimes, it is good to pause and see where you have been in your life. It can provide you with clues as to what is important to you. It can also reveal your interests, passions, gifts, and opportunities for growth.

If you keep a journal, take a trip down memory lane and see what you have captured in your journals over time. I took a trip down memory lane as a part of the writing process. I found that my core values have not changed over the years; however, the way I express them has evolved. For example, independence has always been a core value of mine. It has been expressed in various ways over the course of my life. Financial independence inspired me to begin working at the age of fourteen so that I had the freedom to buy all the things that are important to teenagers such as clothes, shoes, and purses. I also began to save for college because I viewed education as a means of furthering my independence. I started working full time right out of college to be able to take care of myself and live independently.

I strive to be an independent thinker—I keep an open mind, draw my own conclusions, and express my point of view in a way that is true to who I am even if it means standing alone.

I am working toward simplicity as a way life as a means of maintaining a certain level of freedom and independence.

I have come to accept that independence is very much a part of who I am and something that I need to honor across all areas of my life. I have learned to embrace and express this core value more fully as I have matured.

There are a number of resources (e.g., life coaches, spiritual directors) to help facilitate your inner journey and the process of honoring your values and listening to inner guidance.

Self-knowledge and self-acceptance will help you unlock your potential and create a life that is true to you.

VISION STATEMENT

You will eventually want to create a vision statement that describes how you want to live your life based on your values, gifts/talents, passions, and abilities.

Creating a vision statement is an iterative process. Write down some initial thoughts and keep working at it until your statement resonates with you. Your vision statement should serve as a source of inspiration and a light that guides your way.

◆ ◆ ◆

Embrace your power and your purpose, and expect the best for your life.

FAITH

Faith is looking forward with positive expectancy. It is belief plus trust in divine possibility. Faith is more than saying, "I believe." True faith is demonstrated through commitment and action even if you cannot see exactly where you are going. Truth is the light that guides your way. Trust inspires action.

When expectations are rooted in spiritual faith, we proactively pursue our personal dreams from a deep sense of connection to a greater plan and purpose. The future is embraced as potential and possibility. We hope for the best and move into action in anticipation that our expectations will be fulfilled.

If things do not go as planned, spiritual faith enables us to look for the lesson and trust there is a greater plan at work in our lives. The gift of faith is vision: the ability to see beyond what is to what could be.

Spiritual faith is an ever-renewing source of strength, hope, and enlightenment.

Questions for Reflection
What are you expecting for your life?
What lessons have you learned as a result of your expectations not being fulfilled?
What is one thing you can do over the next thirty days to embrace your power and purpose?

> Take the first step in faith. You don't have to
> see the whole staircase, just take the first step.
>
> — Dr. Martin Luther King Jr.

CHAPTER 2

BE FRUITFUL

◆ ◆ ◆

PURPOSE-DRIVEN PRODUCTIVITY

FRUITFULNESS IS ENABLED THROUGH A strong personal foundation, a root system that enables you to bear "fruit" that is true to you.

Knowing your core values, having structure in your life, and living fully in the present will help you build a strong foundation for success.

LIFE ASSESSMENT

I invite you to take some time to evaluate where you are in your life and where you would like to be. The gap in between represents a golden opportunity for personal development and growth. Think of growth in terms of current opportunities and future possibilities. There may be things you need to do in the short term to enable you to pursue longer-term goals.

Be truthful about where you are without getting stuck in feelings of guilt or regret. Honor your feelings, and make a note of where in your life you have feelings of guilt or regret, but do not let it stop you from working through the exercise.

You will be conducting a holistic assessment of your life. Please feel free to modify the list of life dimensions as appropriate. This exercise is best accomplished in writing.

Life Dimension	Where am I?	Gap	Where would I like to be?	Why?
Health and Fitness				
Relationships (Personal and Professional)				
Career/Profession				
Finances				
Creative Expression				
Spiritual Fulfillment/ Contribution				
Travel and Entertainment				
Physical Environments (Home, Car, Office)				

STEP ONE

Key question: Where am I?

Be as specific as possible when establishing where you are with subjective and objective measures. For example, a subjective assessment of health and fitness would be, "I feel tired all the time," or "I am unable to walk a flight of stairs without feeling winded." An objective assessment would be, "I weigh two hundred pounds."

Establishing where you are in life grounds you in reality and answers the question regarding what is true about your life right now. It gives you a starting point from which to move forward. The best place to start making changes is where you are right now.

Evaluate your level of satisfaction with the key areas of your life. Place an X in the column that best represents your level of satisfaction at this time.

1 = not at all satisfied

5 = extremely satisfied

Life Dimension	1	2	3	4	5
Health and Fitness					
Relationships (Personal and Professional)					
Career/Profession					
Finances					

Creative Expression					
Spiritual Fulfillment/ Contribution					
Travel and Entertainment					
Physical Environments (Home, Car, Office)					

In which areas are you most satisfied? Why? In which areas are you least satisfied? Why? Are there any themes or patterns related to the areas in which you feel satisfied or dissatisfied?

STEP TWO

Key question: Where would I like to be in a specified period of time?

Choose a time frame that works best for you right now (e.g., thirty days, ninety days, one year, five years, etc.). You can always come back to this exercise and work through another time frame. If you are new to setting goals, try a ninety-day time frame to start.

What does success look like? Describe where you would like to be in the time frame that you have chosen. Describe your desire in detail.

Create a clear statement of the desired outcome. This statement represents your goal. Goals keep your mind focused and your life moving forward.

Consider using images and/or symbols as a visual representation of your desired outcome. Images and symbols are the language of the soul. Visual representations of your desired outcome are also known as treasure maps and vision boards.

STEP THREE

Key question: Why do I want this for my life? Evaluate each goal.

What core value or values is this outcome connected to? How is the goal connected to your passions, gifts/talents, and abilities? How does this outcome support your vision of success? Overall, do your goals help you achieve what is most important to you?

This step is best accomplished with your responses to the questions in chapter 1, particularly the values exercise.

You are more likely to persevere in the face of obstacles and setbacks if you are pursuing goals that are clearly linked to who you are and what is most important to you. Your goals should enable you to bear "fruit" that is true to you.

STEP FOUR

Key question: What is my opportunity for growth? Evaluate each goal.

How big is the gap between where you are and where you would like to be? How does the gap make you feel? What is needed to close the gap?

The gap provides a wealth of information. Take your time identifying your opportunities for growth. Think in terms of current opportunities and future possibilities.

For example, a current opportunity might be paying off debt to enable you to qualify for a mortgage to purchase your dream home. Another example might be enrolling in school or a training program to enable you to pursue a career that you love.

The gap could highlight areas where you need more structure in your life or more attention to the routine aspects of life. For example, you may need to improve your organizational skills or create a schedule to clean your home or pay your bills.

I encourage you to embrace the gap as an opportunity for personal growth. Think about who you need to become as well as what you need to do to close the gap.

STEP FIVE

Key question: What am I committed to changing and why?

- I suggest you focus on one to two areas of your life versus trying to overhaul your entire life.
- You will find that focusing on one to two key areas will also positively impact other areas of your life.
- Consider the areas in which you are least satisfied with your life as areas of opportunity.
- Make a commitment to yourself in writing.

We tend to think of commitments as something that we make to other people. The real test of your ability to commit is your ability to commit to yourself. It is through our own commitment to loving, honoring, and valuing ourselves that we are able to genuinely commit to others. True commitments flow from your heart and pull you forward.

If there are gaps between your commitments and actions, see it as an opportunity for personal growth rather than a personal failing. Recommit to your goals, and begin again.

Step six

Create a compelling plan of action that outlines in detail how you intend to close the gap between where you are and where you would like to be. An effective plan includes the resources that are needed to accomplish your goal, actions that you will take in pursuit of your goals, milestones, and timing for completion.

Expect to face challenges and obstacles along the way, and plan for it. Cultivate patience to see your dreams come to life.

Step seven

Get into action, and measure your progress. Measuring your results will keep you accountable. It will also help you identify where you need to make adjustments to your plan.

Stay open to guidance during the process, and trust that you are being guided to your highest good.

Get support from *like-minded* friends and family. Try not to share your goals with people who cannot genuinely support you. It will drain your energy and diminish your enthusiasm.

◆ ◆ ◆

Courage to Change

Be the change you wish to see in the world.

— Mohandas Gandhi

It takes courage to make changes in our lives. We create change by focusing our attention on what we have the power to change—ourselves!

In my younger years, I thought I had the power to change others. What I have learned over the years is that we can influence others, but true lasting change must come from within. We can support another person's growth, but we cannot own their growth or force them to change.

Inspire others through your commitment to your own personal development and growth. Try not to approach your development from a place of deficit. You are not broken, and you do not need to be "fixed." Start where you are right now and trust the process.

Your power to change your life is in the present through your choices and action. You have the power to choose what is true for you.

There is no substitute for doing your inner work. Reading books and attending workshops are great personal development tools; however, you ultimately have to do your own inner work.

Purpose-driven productivity will enable you to fulfill the vision that you have created for your life.

◆ ◆ ◆

SERVICE/CONTRIBUTION

Service is purpose-driven productivity at its best. It is a natural outgrowth of your connection to your higher purpose. There are many ways to serve (e.g., community, church, specific causes, etc.). It can take the form of time, talent, and/or financial resources.

I have served/contributed in different ways over the years based on where my heart has led me. I have a deep appreciation for the transforming power of prayer. I served my spiritual community through its prayer ministry for several years. It was my gift to the community with no expectation of return, and yet I received so much as a result of being in service to others. I grew in my own capacity for love and compassion through the experience of praying with others. I am forever connected to the ministry and the community through this sacred service.

Education and learning are also core values that have inspired me to regularly contribute to two organizations that support teachers and students. It is my way of paying it forward in a manner that is connected to my heart.

When you are deeply connected to your purpose, service is a way to contribute to the greater good with no expectation of return. You will be naturally drawn to organizations, people, causes, and so on that align with your purpose. Let your heart be your guide.

CHAPTER 3

BE THANKFUL

◆ ◆ ◆

GRACE AND GRATITUDE

> If the only prayer you ever say in your
> entire life is thank you, it will
> be enough.
>
> — MEISTER ECKHART

What comes to mind when you hear the phrase "grace of God"? Take a few minutes, and write down what comes to mind.

Some of the responses that I have heard when I have posed this question in workshops include luck, forgiveness, serenity, blessing, free pass, unconditional love, protection, and compassion. As you can see from the responses, "grace of God" is a phrase that has many positive associations. How similar or different are your associations to the responses that I have received in workshops?

The word *grace* is rooted in the Latin word *gratia*, which, in essence, means "something that is pleasing and given unconditionally."

My perception of grace has changed over the years as a result of my own growth process. I used to think of grace as something that showed up in times of need. I mostly associated the idea of grace with the "saving grace" that we often experience in difficult or challenging times. It is through an intentional practice of gratitude that I have come to realize that we live our lives in and through the grace of God.

I am using the term *grace* in the sense of ease, flow, and love. I am not referring to emotional/conditional love. I am referring to spiritual/unconditional love that nurtures, guides, sustains, and protects us. It is the type of love that is hard to define and describe, because it surpasses all understanding.

Awakening to the power and presence of grace in my life has given me a feeling of being deeply loved and divinely assisted as I journey through life.

Grace is a spiritual gift. We do not have to earn it or prove that we are worthy of receiving it. It is omnipresent and always at work in our lives—nurturing, guiding, sustaining, and protecting us.

Can you think of a time when you have felt divinely guided toward or away from something? Or a time when you felt a deep sense of peace and contentment when there was chaos and confusion all around you? That is the energy of grace working in and through your life.

I had one of the most transformative experiences of grace through the dream that I shared in the introduction. The energy that I felt in my dream was like nothing I had ever experienced before; it was warm and profoundly loving. It touched my soul in a way that is indescribable. It awakened me and helped me move forward.

I believe we awaken to the power and presence of grace through life experiences and learn to trust that it is always at work in our lives.

AMAZING GRACE

I would be remiss in writing about the grace of God without mentioning one of the most beloved songs about grace. "Amazing Grace," written by John Newton, is a heartfelt song about the power of what is often referred to as redemptive grace.

I have always loved the song, but I gained a deeper appreciation for it after I learned the backstory that inspired it. I also had the opportunity to see the Broadway musical that brought the story to life.

Mr. Newton was involved in the African slave trade through his maritime profession and living the life of a self-professed "wretch." Through his travels, he experienced a number of challenging situations that eventually motivated him to seek assistance from a higher place. He credited the change in his beliefs about slavery and his line of work to the grace of God. The transformation that began in his soul ultimately changed the way he lived.

Mr. Newton, in essence, had a spiritual awakening that helped him to see his choices and actions in a different light. He gained spiritual sight through his awakening. He was no longer "blind" to the impact of his choices and actions on others. Spiritual sight is insight and understanding that inspires action.

I am grateful that Mr. Newton was inspired to share his experience of being transformed through the power of grace. His transformation has helped to free, heal, comfort, and inspire others.

I like to think that we are transformed from our "wretched" and misguided ways through the power of grace. It is the energy of the most transformative power—love.

We experience grace on many levels and in many different ways. It might be experienced as support, guidance, strength, protection, or other ways, depending on the situation. It works in mysterious ways and is often recognized in hindsight. If you have ever looked back on a difficult time in your life and wondered how you made it through, know that grace was at work in your life.

The well-known poem "Footprints in the Sand" captures the essence of grace during challenging times. In the poem, the experience of grace is highlighted as being carried during difficult times. The poem is a great reminder that we are not alone and that the power, presence, and grace of God is greater than any circumstance that we may face.

Questions for Reflection
How have you experienced God's grace in your life?
What have been some of your "amazing grace" moments?

Gratitude
We can raise our awareness of how grace is always at work in our lives through an intentional practice of experiencing and expressing gratitude.

The word *gratitude* is also rooted in the Latin word *gratia*. I think of gratitude as recognition of the gift of grace working in and through our lives. Simply stated, gratitude is giving heartfelt thanks for everything that has been provided to you. It can be a formal or informal practice. The benefit of making it a formal practice is that it enables you to review and reflect on your thoughts at different periods of your life. It also helps you slow down to allow the feeling of gratitude to move through you and connect your head with your heart.

I have found that beginning and ending each day in a spirit of gratitude is a life-changing practice. It has helped me to see how truly blessed I am each and every day. It has helped me shift my focus from what is missing from life to the abundant blessings in my life.

I believe that giving thanks for blessings as well as challenges is the most transformative practice. It will give you a greater perspective and help you to cultivate spiritual sight.

It is easy to be thankful when things are going your way and all is well by most standards; however, to give thanks only for what you perceive as positive in your life is to miss an opportunity for transformation and growth. It is much harder to give thanks when you are faced with a difficult situation/circumstance or when you perceive that your prayers have gone unanswered.

Gratitude in the midst of difficulty and disappointment requires faith in a higher plan and purpose at work in your life. It is a practice of openness and trust. Your level of trust in life will influence how you experience life.

Turning points are often a result of a new level of understanding of self, others, or a situation. Can you think of a difficult situation/circumstance you faced or a time when you felt a prayer went unanswered, and it turned out to be a turning point in your life? What did you learn from the experience? How did you grow from it? What new opportunity did it provide you? How did your life change as a result?

A daily practice of gratitude is a wonderful way to see how grace is working in and through your life each and every day. It will increase your appreciation for the life that you have right now even if it is not your ideal life. It will help you cultivate a mind-set of abundance that will take root and blossom in your life.

Taking a few minutes in the morning to give heartfelt thanks for the gift of a new day is a great way to start the day. An ongoing evening practice of reflecting on the day and writing three to five things you consider gifts, blessings, challenges, or life lessons in a journal or notebook will transform the way you experience your day and your life.

Review your list from time to time so you can see how grace is working in and through your life. A grateful heart is an open heart and a channel for grace, the energy of spiritual/unconditional love, to flow through you to others. Extending love and compassion to others is a natural outgrowth of your own self-love and self-compassion.

You are blessed beyond measure through the gift of grace.

QUESTIONS FOR REFLECTION
Who or what has been your greatest blessing?
How are you a blessing to others?

SUGGESTIONS

- Begin and end your day in gratitude.
- Give thanks for gifts, blessings, challenges, and life lessons.

 * When faced with challenges, ask yourself the
   following:
     o What can I learn from this experience?
     o How can I grow from this experience?
 * Affirm abundant blessings.
 * Extend gratitude to others.

CHAPTER 4

BE WILLING TO LET GO

◆ ◆ ◆

RELEASE LIMITING BELIEFS, THE PAST, AND WHAT IS COMPLETE

LETTING GO OF THINGS THAT no longer serve your highest good is a spiritual practice that enables you to make room for new beginnings, new opportunities, and new blessings. It is a process that is forward looking with positive expectancy.

RELEASE LIMITING BELIEFS

The nature of life is change and transition for the purpose of growth and evolution.

We can begin a new chapter in our lives any time we are willing to open our minds to new possibilities and truly believe that we are worth the change that we seek.

Beliefs are powerful things; they are the vehicles through which we create our lives and filter our experiences. Whatever we believe to be true is the reality from which we create our lives.

As I expressed in the introduction, I lived my life from a core belief that I was fundamentally flawed for many years. I allowed that belief to define me and bind me to a negative self-image for so long. It resulted in my living from a place of fear and insecurity that influenced many choices I made for my life.

It was through a life-changing dream and a willingness to change my beliefs that I stopped trying to fix myself and started exploring what was true for me from a higher, spiritual perspective.

We open the doors to new possibilities when we are willing to release/let go of beliefs that limit us and replace them with beliefs that empower us to create the kind of lives and world that we desire.

Limiting beliefs are often rooted in fear. Fear will disempower you and keep you from pursuing what you truly desire. It can also shift you into a mode of control to protect yourself. When you are in protection mode, you are closed. You are, in essence, blocking your blessings and guidance from a higher place.

Fear is an emotion that is a part of life; however, it does not have to rule your life. Bringing awareness to what you fear can help you put your fears in perspective and help you move to a more desired state.

EXERCISE
What do you fear? Make a list of fears.

What is the root of each of your fears? Why is it a fear? For example, was there a particular experience that made you fearful, or is it a fear that was passed on to you?

- The root of my fear is…
- It is a fear because...

What is the opposite of each of your fears? For example, if rejection is one of your fears, acceptance is the opposite.

Rejection ⟶ Acceptance

- The opposite of my fear is…

Define the opposite of your fear in terms of what it would mean to you overall and in a particular situation that you are facing. Using acceptance as the example:

- Acceptance is…

What would you need to believe to move away from each of the fears you identified toward a more desired state? Using the previous example:

- I would need to believe _____ to move away from a fear of rejection toward a feeling of acceptance.

What action can you take to move away from the fear you identified toward a more desired state? Using the previous example:

❀ I can _____ to move away from the fear of rejection and move toward a feeling of acceptance.

The opposite of fear is courage, inner strength, and confidence to choose what is best for your own life. You have the power to change your life by changing the beliefs that you hold in your mind. All change in the physical world begins with a change in the mind.

Depending on the situation, it may be appropriate to seek assistance (e.g., a counselor, therapist, minister, etc.) to help you work through your fears.

AFFIRMATIONS

An intentional practice of affirming life-enhancing beliefs will help you focus your mind on creating the life that you truly desire.

Affirmations are positive statements that help you replace limiting beliefs with empowering beliefs. Replacing, not just trying to eliminate, limiting beliefs is critical to making changes in your life. It helps you shift your thought process and your focus. I believe affirmations are most powerful when they are written in your own words. You will want to repeat them often to focus your mind.

Your mind is fertile ground. The seeds that you choose to plant and nurture each day will take root and blossom in your life.

EXERCISE

Create a few affirmations that will help you focus your mind on building the life that you desire.

Examples of affirmations are as follows:

- ❧ I live my truth.
- ❧ I am divinely guided.
- ❧ I am blessed.
- ❧ I choose what is best for my life.
- ❧ I am stepping into my power.
- ❧ I trust the process.

◆ ◆ ◆

BE WILLING TO LET GO OF THE PAST

Forgiveness is a process of releasing the past in a spirit of truth and acceptance. Truth has the power to heal and transform our lives. It is the light that guides our way.

I appreciate the art of storytelling through live theater and motion pictures. I saw a great example of standing in truth a few years ago in the movie *Flight*, starring Denzel Washington. About halfway through the movie, I started questioning my sanity for wanting to see a movie concerning a plane crash. I was a relatively frequent flyer at the time, and I did not need any reminders about all the things that could go wrong on a flight. However, by the end of the movie, I realized that it had much less to do with a plane crash and more to do with standing in truth. The crash was merely a catalyst for change in the life of the protagonist.

There was a point in the movie when Washington's character had a life-altering moment of truth that came in the form of a public admission of a deeply personal issue that had kept him in bondage. He had a serious substance abuse problem.

Prior to his admission, Washington's character cried out, "God help me." It was an intense and extremely powerful scene in the movie. His internal struggle to tell the truth was painfully apparent.

The scene in the movie was an act of surrender that allowed him to stand in the truth of the situation so that he could move forward. The truth was not without serious consequences. He went to jail, which is physical confinement, but his soul was free from the bondage of abuse, lies, and past wrongdoings.

Although I do not have personal experience with the substance abuse issue that Washington's character faced in the movie, I related to the feeling of freedom that comes from acknowledging and accepting a painful truth to be able to move forward in life.

The story line in *Flight* is a great reminder of the power of truth to change and heal our lives. We cannot change what we do not acknowledge and truly accept.

I used to think of acceptance as defeat or resignation; however, I now think of acceptance as letting go with faith that there is a higher plan and purpose at work in my life.

Instead of looking back on challenging or painful situations with regret, I am learning to look back and ask what I learned from the situation and how the lesson learned can serve me in the future.

Focusing on past mistakes, hurts, missed opportunities, or the wrongs of others is a dead-end focus that will keep you anchored in the past.

When we let go of the past, we make room for new beginnings, new opportunities, and new blessings in our lives, and we live fully in the present.

Sometimes we are still unknowingly bound to the past in spite of forgiveness work. I had a forgiveness issue show up for me when I received my ancestry DNA results. In addition to having African DNA, I have British DNA and other European DNA in my bloodline. Based on what we know about slavery, there is no mystery as to how the mixing of bloodlines occurred.

I unexpectedly felt a deep sense of sadness and anger the day I received the results. I was not surprised by the results, because I know my family's history; however, there was something about seeing evidence of my bloodline in writing that stirred deep and painful emotions.

I thought about my ancestors being captured like wild animals, enslaved, mistreated, raped, and dehumanized. The more I thought about it, the angrier I became. It made me realize that I still had unprocessed feelings about slavery. My DNA results were a catalyst for those feelings to come to the surface so that they could be acknowledged and addressed.

Forgiveness does not mean that the past does not matter or that we have not experienced pain, hurt, or disappointment. It is acceptance that we cannot change the past, and we are releasing it in order to move forward. The gift of forgiveness is freedom from circumstances that bind us to the past.

Forgiveness is not just about forgiving others; it is also about forgiving yourself. If you are not able to forgive yourself, it is not likely that you will be able to genuinely forgive others.

Depending on the situation, it may be appropriate to seek assistance (e.g., a counselor, therapist, minister, etc.) to help you work through forgiveness.

QUESTIONS FOR REFLECTION
Who or what do I need to forgive?
What do I need to release to move forward?
What action can I take to move forward?

❖ ❖ ❖

Be Willing to Let Go of What Is Complete in Your Life

The circle of life is a process of growth and evolution through a series of beginnings and endings. Endings are a necessary part of life to make room for new beginnings.

Knowing what is complete in your life empowers you to keep moving forward. Being stuck is often the result of not being willing to release something that is complete to make room for something new.

I recently received guidance to make room for a new beginning as it pertains to my career. I was sitting in silence contemplating my next career move. I had reached a career crossroads, and for the first time, I wasn't sure of the next steps. The only thing I knew for certain was that another corporate job was not my immediate next step. That was a radical thought for someone who had spent the past twenty-five-plus years working in corporate America. By the end of my time in silence, it was clear to me that I had come to the end of the road at my job and that I needed to create space for something new.

Whenever I would start thinking about how and when I was going to move on, my good friends Ms. Doubt and Ms. Fear would show up with 101 reasons why I needed to stay the course. I allowed doubt and fear of losing my financial independence to keep me at a crossroads for some time.

The guidance I received to create space for something new to emerge tested my sensibilities about independence, work, and money. Independence is one of my core values, and traditional work has always been a means of financial independence. I have been, by choice, working since I was fourteen. It was hard for me to imagine taking a break from what I knew to allow "something" to emerge.

I worked for a good company, and I was committed to my job and my team. However, I knew in my heart that it was time to let go so that I could embrace the next phase of my journey. I had many internal and external clues that it was time to move on.

I felt deeply conflicted and resistant to letting go. This is not the first time that I have felt conflicted at a crossroads, and I am sure it will not be the last either. I am a work in progress. You are, too. We are all works in progress.

I prayerfully decided to leave my job in faith that I was being guided to the next phase of my journey. The space I provided myself allowed this book to emerge and be completed. Parts of it existed in my journals and in my head, but I needed time and space to pull it altogether.

The process of writing this book has been a thousandfold blessing. It has deepened my faith in spiritual guidance. Writing for public consumption is a vulnerable act. I found myself experiencing writer's block when I allowed the fear of judgment to stifle my message. I overcame the blocks by allowing myself to be guided from a higher place.

It has helped me further clarify my own values and, in the process, see how much I have grown over time. The process also deepened my sense of gratitude for the employment I had over the years that allowed me to take a break.

Months later, I can honestly say that I have not looked back on my decision to take a breather from corporate

America with any regrets. It was something that I needed to do as a part of my own growth progress. I managed through the transition with the support of family and friends as well as the principles and practices that I am outlining in this book.

I must admit that I surprisingly felt a bit of an identity crisis at the beginning of my break. I did not realize how much of my identity was tied to my work and employer. Shortly after I left, I was engaged in a conversation that eventually led to a typical question that is asked when someone is getting to know you: "What do you do?" It was in that moment that I surprisingly felt a bit of a void in my existence. I was used to having a title and a company to give as a response. It was a part of my identity. I felt a sense of loss for a bit, but eventually this void shifted to a feeling of excitement about a new beginning. I would describe my journey to date as a process of further simplifying my life and honoring what is most important to me.

I shared this personal example of an ending to highlight the power of releasing what is complete in your life in faith that you are being guided to your highest good.

The caterpillar's journey to becoming a butterfly is a wonderful metaphor about letting go of what is complete to embrace the next phase of the journey.

I had an opportunity to foster a caterpillar's transition to a butterfly during the writing of this book. I have seen the transition on television over the years through documentaries, but there is nothing like being a witness to the actual process.

Butterfly image by Matt Gomez.

The caterpillar's journey to becoming a butterfly begins when it responds/surrenders to an internal urge to grow and evolve. Before a caterpillar creates its cocoon, a sacred space to be transformed, it hangs upside down for about twenty-four hours without any movement. Its period of stillness ends with the shedding of its skin for the last time. The shedding of its skin (old self) enables the caterpillar to create a cocoon in which it completely dissolves and is re-created into a butterfly. The butterfly remains in the cocoon for ten to fourteen days, emerges, pumps up its wings, and eventually takes flight. It is truly a magical and purpose-driven process.

As winged creatures, butterflies contribute to the reproductive cycle of flowers through the process of pollination. The caterpillar has to be transformed to serve a higher purpose. The caterpillar's journey to becoming a butterfly is a great reminder that we need to respond to our inner urges/promptings to grow and evolve to serve a higher purpose.

The caterpillar's journey to becoming a butterfly is also a reminder about the importance of balance as we journey through life. There are periods of activity as well as periods of rest throughout the process.

We obviously do not go through the type of transformation that a caterpillar does to become a butterfly, but through our own growth process, we are born again and again into higher states of consciousness that enable us to serve a higher purpose and experience life more fully.

Our challenge is to trust the process and be willing to embrace endings as gateways to new beginnings.

QUESTIONS FOR REFLECTION

Is there something in your life that is complete and in need of release?

What is one thing that you can do to begin the process of releasing what is complete so that you can embrace the next phase of your journey?

CHAPTER 5

BE STILL

◆ ◆ ◆

REST AND RENEWAL

TAKING TIME TO BE STILL is just as important as taking action. Being still is a powerful tool of renewal. It helps us cultivate patience, presence, openness, trust, and balance.

One of the lessons I learned through the dream that I shared in the introduction was the power of being still. I spent a great deal of time in my dream going from room to room looking for the dog that I thought I had neglected. Every room that I entered was filled with clutter. It wasn't until I reached the last room and rested that I had a breakthrough. Unlike the other rooms in my dream, the last room was completely empty except for a bed. It was a sacred space for me to be still and open to guidance.

PRAYER

It was a simple prayer in the middle of the night that prompted my dream and opened the door for spiritual renewal. I believe that prayer is one of the most important spiritual practices. It is a universal act of communion that is rooted in openness and trust in a divine source.

A personal prayer practice builds self-discipline and increases spiritual awareness and openness to spiritual guidance. It enables you to hear your spiritual voice of truth more clearly.

Most people associate prayer with talking; however, I have found that prayer is not so much about words as it is intention and a genuine connection to your spiritual source. A prayer that is felt deeply in your heart and never spoken out loud is much more powerful than a spoken prayer that has no personal meaning.

One of the most important shifts that I made in my prayer practice was a shift from focusing on my problems and needs to expressing gratitude and listening to spiritual guidance. Prior to the shift in my practice, my prayers took the form of pleading and bargaining or reciting prayers that did not have any personal meaning.

The catalyst for the shift in my prayer practice was a shift in my beliefs about God. I do not think of God as a man/person who grants favors or seeks to punish. I think of God as a divine presence working in and through my life.

I feel a deep sense of gratitude in prayer because I know that if not for this divine presence, I would not have life.

It is important to explore your beliefs about God (or whatever word you use for your spiritual source) because it will affect how you pray. If you believe God can be manipulated through prayer, your prayers will reflect that belief. You will more than likely beg/plead for things and make promises that you cannot keep in exchange for getting what you want. This type of approach will likely lead you to conclude that prayer is ineffective.

The purpose of prayer is not to change God but rather, to change us from inside out through spiritual awareness and guidance.

I believe we are continuously being called into divine communion. The call may take the form of restlessness, impatience, or a challenging situation. I felt a deep sense of longing for many years that I could not articulate. I now know that it was a call to a deeper and more spiritual way of life.

Prayer is your answer to a divine call to live from your spiritual core—your center of truth and authenticity.

My commitment to a daily prayer practice has without a doubt been one of the most challenging and fulfilling commitments I have made in my life. I would go so far as to say that it has altered the course of my life.

HEART-CENTERED PRAYER

Heart-centered prayer is a wonderful way to be still and open to guidance. It is a prayer practice that is meditative in nature and practiced in silence. When you are centered in your heart, there is no reason for spoken words. There is communication in the act of being still and silent. It expresses openness and trust in your spiritual source.

The goal of heart-centered prayer is to stay fully present in the moment. It will enable you to clearly hear your spiritual voice of truth.

Heart-centered prayer helps you cultivate the qualities of patience, presence, openness, and trust.

To begin, sit comfortably in an upright position, and take a few cleansing breaths. Once you have relaxed, set an intention to be still and to trust the process. Use a heart-centered word (e.g., truth, trust, grace, peace, love, etc.) and/or your breath as a focal point for your practice. My suggestion is to choose a word that you are going to use before you begin this practice and stick with it for a while. I silently speak my heart-centered word when I feel distracted.

I encourage you to center yourself in silence as a part of your daily routine. Strive for fifteen to twenty minutes in silence. If fifteen to twenty minutes seem overwhelming, start with five minutes or whatever amount of time feels right to you. Set a timer so that you can be fully present in the moment and not watching the clock.

Conclude your time in silence with gratitude, and capture your experience in your notebook or journal.

A prayer journal is a wonderful way to deepen your experience of prayer through the written word. It is a vehicle for reflection and personal expression within the context of communion and sacred time. The journal can include formal and informal prayers, scriptures, inspirational quotes, and other items that have special meaning to your life.

I was inspired to write a personal commitment to my journey that has become a daily prayer.

Commitment to the Journey

Thank you for the gift of life and your grace that nurtures, guides, sustains, and protects me. I feel you pulling me closer to you, and I am willing to be led. I commit my mind, body, and spirit to this sacred journey and process of empowerment. I trust you are guiding my steps. I say yes to your dream of wholeness and oneness. Yes, and amen!

I invite you to write a commitment to your own journey. I suggest you review your commitment each morning as part of your routine.

Thinking of life as a journey will help you maintain a sense of wonder and adventure.

Questions for Reflection

What is the purpose of prayer?

Why do you or don't you pray?

What do you see as the benefits of a daily prayer practice?

❖ ❖ ❖

NIGHTLY RENEWAL

Nighttime is a natural time of stillness. It is a mystical time of day in which we are renewed in mind, body, and spirit. It is a time for us to be still and trust the process.

Have you ever thought about going to sleep as an act of faith? It is. We go to sleep in trust (whether conscious or not) that we will awaken in the morning. Creating a morning practice of giving thanks for the gift of renewal and a new day is a great way to acknowledge the gift of the night.

Our 24-7 lifestyles have taken away from this sacred time of renewal. There was a period in my life when I felt as if my days were running together. I was not doing a good job of balancing my life. Work made up a disproportionate part of my day and my life. I would leave work, go home, and continue to work well past midnight.

Improvements in technology have been both a blessing and a curse. The ability to work from home has many benefits, but it also has many drawbacks such as stress and low energy if we are not able to disconnect from work on a daily basis.

My schedule was not conducive to nightly renewal, and it resulted in being frustrated, uninspired, and burned out by the end of the week. Weekends became a time of recovery instead of a refreshing break.

I realized that I had to make changes in terms of how I was managing my day to ensure that I was getting the adequate amount of rest and renewal on a daily basis. It was impossible to make up for an imbalanced week over the weekend. Believe me, I tried.

We each have to cultivate balance in our lives. It does not happen automatically because we are a part of a society that is out of control and out of balance. Most of us do not have a reality check because we work and associate with people who are also out of balance.

Corporate mergers, reorganizations, and downsizing have many people feeling as if they need to be continuously connected to work and make a lot of personal sacrifices to prove that they are adding value. Downsizing/rightsizing has become a way of life in corporations. There is constant fear of being demoted or being eliminated from an organization. I understand the fear because I have lived it at various points in my career.

Sadly, it does not really matter how many personal sacrifices you make for a corporation when it comes to mergers, acquisitions, reorganizations and downsizing. Employees are a means to an end. When you no longer serve the corporation's end, you have reached your end at that corporation. It is that simple. It is not fair, and it is not right, but that is the reality of the corporate world.

My biggest learning over the course of twenty-five-plus years in the workforce is that it is important to keep work in perspective. It is an important part of life, but it should not be your entire life.

Your health and well-being have to be your own priority. Your personal balance is not your employer's priority, and it is not something that you are going to magically find. It is something that you have to create for yourself through commitment and action.

Health issues are often a wake-up call that something needs to change. I encourage you to pay attention to your body's warning signals that your life is out of balance.

If your life feels out of balance, take the first step in restoring balance through a commitment to nightly renewal. Making small changes each day can make a big difference in your life. I will provide suggestions to enhance this sacred time of renewal in the next chapter.

Explore Your Nighttime Dreams

As long as I can remember, I have been a vivid nighttime dreamer. My dreams have proven to be a great source of information and inspiration for my life.

If you are not already exploring your dreams, you can begin by writing them down, even if you remember only small fragments. I have found that paying attention to my dreams and writing them down enables me to remember them more often and in more detail.

I have also found it helpful to give my dreams a name and draw key elements as I remember them. I was gifted a beautiful painting of a scene from the dream that I shared in the introduction. It reflects the last room I entered, where I encountered my younger self. It is a great reminder of the transforming power of truth and openness to spiritual guidance.

There are a variety of ways to explore your dreams. It is important to research different methods and use the one that best resonates with you. I have personally benefitted from an open-ended approach that explores the imagery and the emotions associated with a dream.

You may also want to consider joining a dream circle for support. The group I participated in supported members by listening to their dreams, exploring the imagery and emotions associated with dreams, and offering interpretations of dreams as if they were their own. It was a safe environment for sharing, exploring, and hearing other interpretations of my dreams. Keep in mind, however, that you are the only person who can truly decide the meaning and significance of your dreams. Your dreams could potentially open a door for spiritual renewal.

Give yourself the gift of renewal through stillness and silence. Silent prayer and a silent night are powerful tools of renewal.

CHAPTER 6

Bring It All Together on a Daily Basis

◆ ◆ ◆

Life in Progress

WE ARE GIVEN THE GIFT of twenty-four hours each day to spend as we choose. It is a gift that we treasure through the choices that we make each and every day.

We give thanks for the gift of time by spending it wisely and in alignment with our deepest values.

Life can pass you by if you are not putting your values into action and moving in the direction of the vision that you have created for your life.

It is important to plan for the future and to live fully in the present. It is my experience that life seems to flow and progress when we are grounded, present, and living life one day at a time.

I was inspired to embrace the circle of life as a template for my day. It is an approach that is grounding and connects me to the natural flow of the day based on the cycle of the sun.

We are intimately connected to nature and depend on its cycles for our growth and well-being. We are in the flow of life when we are consciously connected to the cycles of life that sustain us.

We tend to think about the circle of life as it relates to the course of our lives or as it relates to the seasons; however, we actually live an entire life cycle (beginning, middle, end, and a period of rest/renewal) over the course of the day.

My hope is that you will see the balance and harmony that is inherent in the circle of life and embrace it as a template for your day. The essence of a circle is wholeness and completion—spiritual qualities that enrich our lives.

I invite you to think holistically about your day:

* morning (beginning)
* daytime (middle)
* evening (end)
* nighttime (rest/renewal)

I have illustrated the circle of life on a daily basis using the cardinal compass points. East is the direction of the rising sun and the beginning of the day. Each morning is the beginning of a new life cycle.

Each part of the day has distinct qualities, gifts, spiritual lessons, and opportunities for growth. I have made suggestions for each part of the day.

* Morning: be intentional.
* Daytime: be fruitful.
* Evening: be thankful and willing to let go.
* Nighttime: be still.

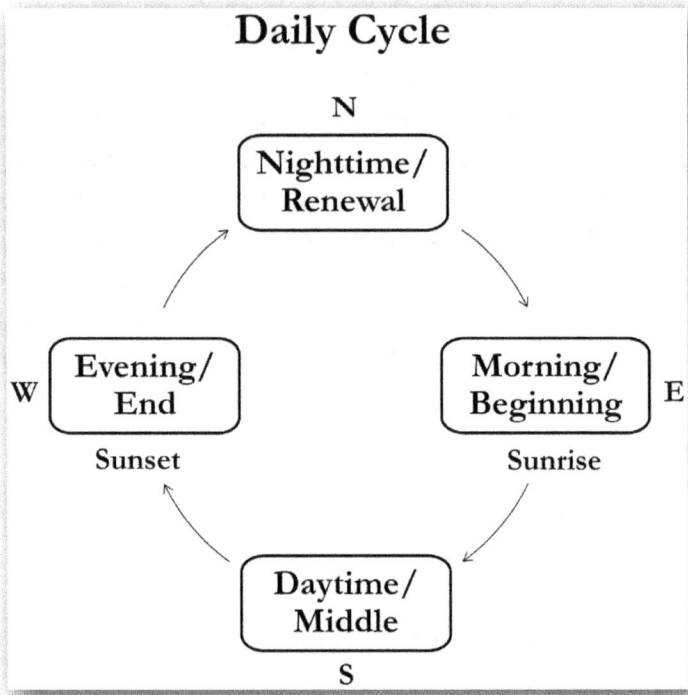

Daily Cycle

N

Nighttime/
Renewal

Evening/
End
W

Morning/
Beginning
E

Sunset

Sunrise

Daytime/
Middle

S

MORNING

Morning is associated with the rising sun, awakening, new beginnings, gratitude, hope, possibility, commitment, vision, and stepping into the light.

Be Intentional

> This is the beginning of a new day. You
> have been given this day to use as you will.
> You can waste it or use it for good. What

you do today is important because you are
exchanging a day of your life for it. When
tomorrow comes, this day will be gone
forever; in its place is something that you
have left behind…Let it be something good.

— ANONYMOUS

Morning suggestions:

* Experience sunrise.
* Step into your power—choose how to spend your day.
* Begin each day with the end in mind—create daily intentions.
* Take a morning walk or do some other grounding activity.
* Express gratitude for the gift of a new day.
* Record your dreams from the night before.
* Center yourself in silence for fifteen minutes.

DAYTIME

Daytime is associated with the sun at its peak, purpose, drive, determination, productivity, contribution, growth, advancement, and progression.

Be Fruitful

Spend time on activities that move your life in the direction of the vision that you have created for your life.

Daytime suggestions:

- Experience the beauty of the daytime sky.
- Make purpose-driven productivity a priority.
- Work your plan of action on a daily basis.
- Pursue your passion.
- Perform daily acts of faith that take you out of your comfort zone.

EVENING

Evening is associated with the setting sun, harvest, gratitude, reflection, fulfillment, contentment, completion, acceptance, and letting go.

Be Willing to Let Go

Evening is a time to bring your day to a close in a spirit of gratitude, peace, and contentment.

Evening suggestions:

- Experience sunset.
- Take an evening walk or do some other grounding activity.
- Review and reflect on your day in the context of your commitments and actions.
- Identify lessons learned.

* Express gratitude for the experiences of the day.
* Practice forgiveness—for yourself and others.
* Declutter/make room for new blessings.
* Prepare for the following day.
* Center yourself in silence for fifteen minutes.

Nighttime

Nighttime is associated with trust, silence, stillness, rest, renewal, revitalization, an inner journey, dreams, the realm of infinite time, space and possibility, and divine mystery.

Be Still

Nighttime is a time to be still. Cherish and protect this time of deep renewal that enables you to begin anew.

Nighttime suggestions:

* Experience the beauty of the night sky.
* Treat nighttime as a sacred time for the deep renewal of your mind, body, and spirit/life force.
* Create an environment that facilitates a peaceful night's sleep and insightful dreams.
* Strive for seven to eight hours of sleep.
* Try to wind down thirty minutes to one hour before going to bed.
* Turn off the phone, television, and computer.

- Choose a loving thought before going to sleep.
- Trust the process.

Daily Balance

Morning and evening are gateways/transition points that help you balance your day.

- Morning is the gateway to daytime.
- Evening is the gateway to nighttime.

I encourage you to create morning and evening routines that enable you to have a hopeful beginning and a peaceful end to your day. It will transform the way you experience your day and your life.

Honoring the circle of life on a daily basis will bring more order and balance and, therefore, harmony into your life. Harmony is a state of peace that is achieved through order and balance.

Thirty-Day Challenge

- Commit to using the circle of life as a template for your day.
- Renew your commitment each day through your thoughts, words, and actions. If there is a gap between your commitment and action, see it as an

opportunity for growth rather than a personal failing. Recommit, and begin again.

❧ Engage the power of the written word to see how you are growing over time.

❧ If you do nothing else, begin and end each day in gratitude. It will transform the way you experience each day and your life.

Parting Thoughts

◆ ◆ ◆

It is my sincere hope that this book has helped you explore what is true for you and begin to put it into action, one day at a time. It is also my hope that you have embraced and experienced the benefits of the principles and practices that have been shared throughout this book.

I encourage you to see life as a work in progress. Stay open to guidance, and trust that you are being guided to your highest good.

I believe that each one of us has something unique and important to bring into the world. There never has been and never will be anyone exactly like you.

Be true to you!

Peace and abundant blessings,

Ruthann

ABOUT THE AUTHOR

◆ ◆ ◆

RUTHANN M. WILSON IS A self-described work in progress. A student of life, she has a passion for personal development that led her to a degree in psychology and training as a life coach. She enjoys helping others pursue their authentic paths through spiritual principles and practices.

In addition to her psychology degree, Ruthann has an MBA with a concentration in management and has held positions of increasing responsibility in corporate America for the past twenty-five years.

With a special interest in spirituality and prayer, Ruthann has supported others through her spiritual community's prayer ministry. She has also led workshops on the power of grace and gratitude. *Be True to You* is her first book.